UNOFFICIAL
STEM CHALLENGES FOR
MINECRAFTERS

GRADES 1–2

SKY PONY PRESS
NEW YORK

Copyright © 2018 by Hollan Publishing, Inc.

Minecraft® is a registered trademark of Notch Development AB.

The Minecraft game is copyright © Mojang AB.

Sky Pony Press books may be purchased in bulk at special discounts for sales promotion, corporate gifts, fund-raising, or educational purposes. Special editions can also be created to specifications. For details, contact the Special Sales Department, Sky Pony Press, 307 West 36th Street, 11th Floor,New York, NY 10018 or info@skyhorsepublishing.com.

Sky Pony® is a registered trademark of Skyhorse Publishing, Inc.®,a Delaware corporation.

Minecraft® is a registered trademark of Notch Development AB. The Minecraft game is copyright © Mojang AB.

Visit our website at www.skyponypress.com.

Authors, books, and more at SkyPonyPressBlog.com.

10 9 8 7 6 5 4 3 2 1

Library of Congress Cataloging-in-Publication Data is available on file.

Cover design by Brian Peterson

Interior design by Joanna Williams

STEM challenges by Aimee Chase

Cover and interior art by Amanda Brack or used by permission from Shutterstock.com.

Print ISBN: 978-1-5107-3757-0

Printed in China

A NOTE TO PARENTS

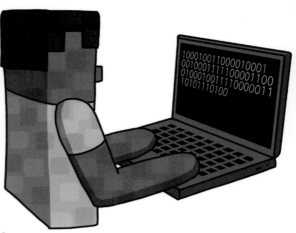

STEM CHALLENGES FOR MINECRAFTERS IS JUST WHAT YOU AND YOUR CHILD HAVE BEEN WAITING FOR, an educational workbook that doesn't feel like an educational workbook. This colorfully illustrated, video game-themed learning tool is focused on four critical domains for young, twenty-first-century learners: ***SCIENCE, TECHNOLOGY, ENGINEERING,*** and ***MATH.*** These content areas can be taught in isolation, but teaching them together (using diamond swords, zombies, creepers, and redstone traps for added fun) allows for deeper understanding and authentic connections to the world where kids live (and play).

Children won't need to be nagged to dive headfirst into this collection of over thirty STEM challenges. Each lesson is designed to develop creativity, critical thinking, and problem-solving skills in kids who can't get enough of their favorite video game. Stand back as they begin to take risks, form theories, and pose unique solutions to complex real-world problems.

Whether they're learning about binary code, algebra, states of matter, or architectural design, they're ***FINDING NEW INTERESTS AND BUILDING CONFIDENCE*** in the classroom and beyond.

GET READY FOR A BRAIN-BUILDING STEM ADVENTURE!

To make a painting in Minecraft, you have to arrange sticks and a white block of wool on a crafting table just like this one.

COOL, RIGHT?

What do you need to make a painting in the real world?
LIST THE MATERIALS BELOW:

DEDUCTIVE REASONING

Steve made lots of paintings today. One of the paintings is hiding the entrance to his **SECRET ROOM** filled with emeralds! Read the clues to find out which one it is!

1. Cross out all the paintings with people in them.

2. Cross out the paintings that have red in them.

3. The painting that's left is hiding a secret room! Circle it.

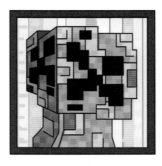

SOLVING

Alex is battling ghasts in the Nether, so she needs a tool or weapon.

It's up to YOU to **INVENT A TOOL** that can help her win the battle *and* protect her from the flaming hot fireballs the ghasts are spitting at her. **DRAW IT IN THE PICTURE BELOW.**

EXPLAIN YOUR INVENTION HERE.

My tool is called a

It is made out of

because

This is how it works:

INVESTIGATING SOUND WAVES

Steve is crafting a shelter when he hears **THREE VERY SCARY SOUNDS.** One is a zombie moaning, another is a ghast shrieking, and the third is a creeper hissing like a snake.

Sound is caused by vibration. It travels in waves like this.

DRAW THE SOUND WAVES MOVING FROM EACH MINECRAFT MOB'S MOUTH TO STEVE'S EARS.

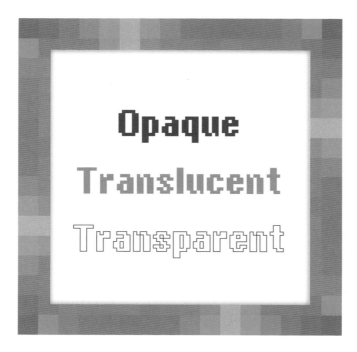

What happens when light hits different materials?

If the material is **OPAQUE,** like a wooden sign, light cannot pass through.

If the material is **TRANSLUCENT,** like apple juice, then some light can pass through it.

If the material is **TRANSPARENT,** like a glass window, light can easily pass through, and you can see objects on the other side.

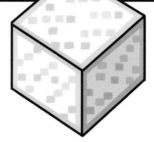

LOOK AROUND AND MAKE A LIST OF ITEMS OR MATERIALS IN YOUR HOME THAT ARE . . .

transparent:

translucent:

opaque:

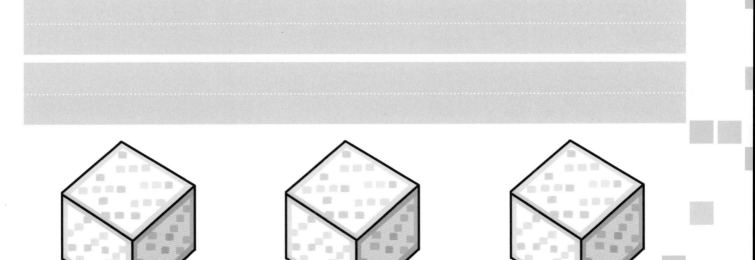

ENGINEERING AND DESIGN

Steve wants to build a shelter that is **MOSTLY OPAQUE** but has a **TRANSPARENT WINDOW.** That way, he has a perfect view of any hostile mobs (like skeletons!) that might approach his home.

CIRCLE THE SHELTER THAT WOULD BE BEST FOR STEVE.

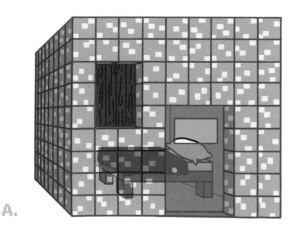

A.

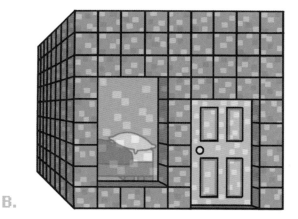

B.

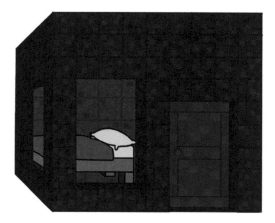

C.

If you play Minecraft, you know that **ZOMBIES BURN UP IN DAYLIGHT!** They like to stay in the dark where they are safe.

DESIGN A HOUSE THAT WOULD BE GREAT FOR A ZOMBIE.

Label the materials you use as opaque, translucent, or transparent!

INSIDE TECHNOLOGY: PIXEL POWER

Images that appear on a computer screen are nothing more than neat rows of equally-sized shapes, like squares. These shapes each have one color and are called **PIXELS**. If you zoom in really close on your favorite video game character, you might be able to see the separate pixels.

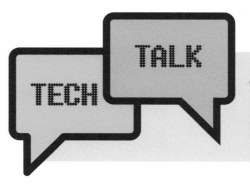

TECH TALK

The word 'pixel' is short for picture element.

COLOR IN THE SQUARE PIXELS OF THE PUFFERFISH BELOW TO MATCH IT TO THE PICTURE AS BEST AS YOU CAN.

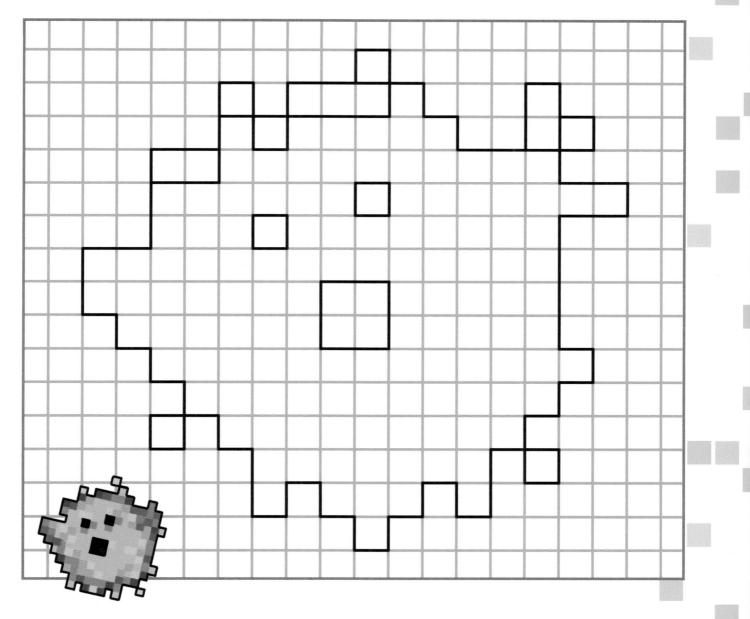

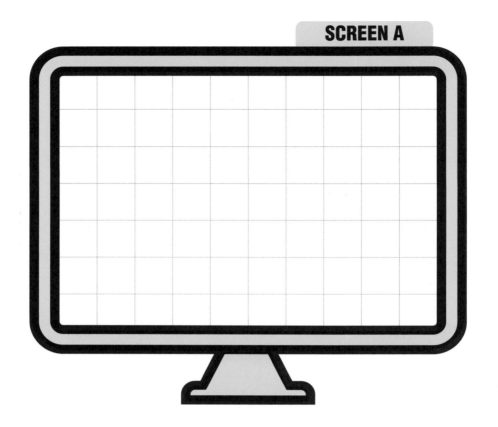

SCREEN A

DRAW YOUR FAVORITE MINECRAFTING WEAPON
or **TOOL** on this computer screen. Color it in,
adding only one color to each (square) pixel.

HOW DID IT COME OUT?

DRAW THE SAME ITEM on the screen at right. Color it
in using only one color for each (square) pixel.

SCREEN B

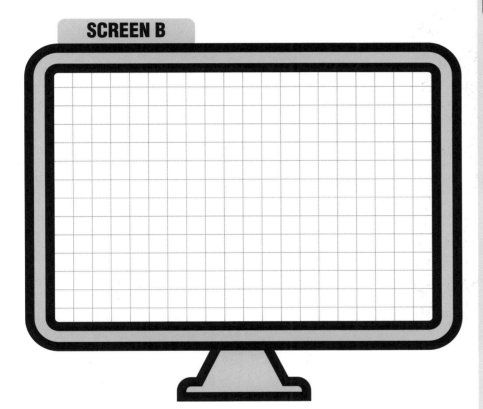

HIGH RESOLUTION:
This phrase describes an image with a lot of pixels. This kind of image is clear to see with lots of details.

LOW RESOLUTION:
This phrase describes an image that might appear a little "fuzzier." It has fewer pixels and less detail.

WHICH SCREEN HAS MORE PIXELS?

Which screen would you use if you wanted to show more detail? Why?

CODE CRACKER: ENCHANTED CHEST

Steve is exploring a cave when he discovers an **ENCHANTED BOOK** inside a secret chest. It holds a very important secret about Minecrafting, but it's **WRITTEN IN CODE.** Help Steve **DECODE THE MESSAGE.**

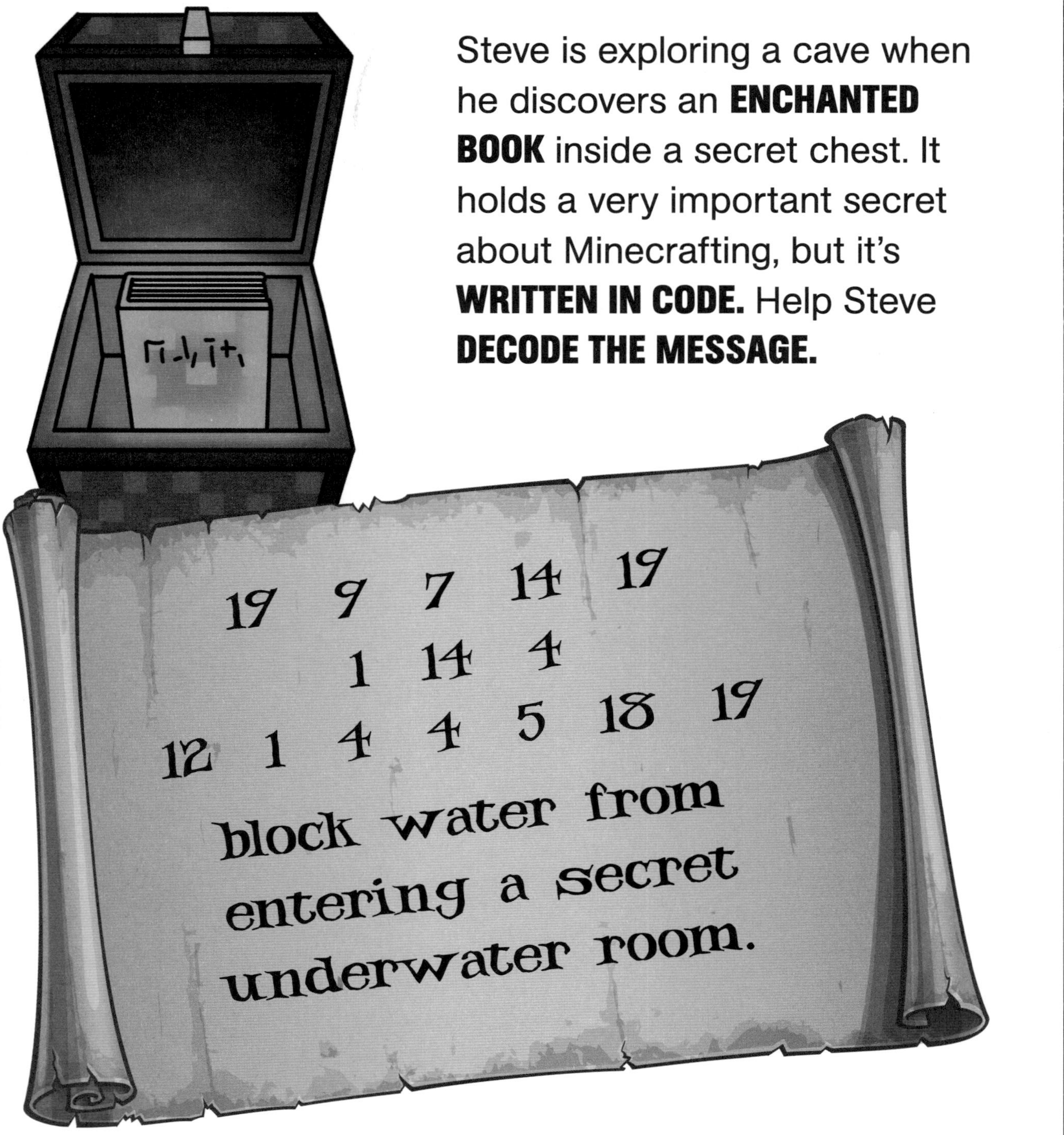

19 9 7 14 19

1 14 4

12 1 4 4 5 18 19

block water from entering a secret underwater room.

The numbers on the scroll each represent a letter of the alphabet and its order in the alphabet. For example, **1=A**. **DECODE THE MESSAGE.**

USE THE KEY BELOW TO HELP YOU.

A	B	C	D	E	F
1	2	3	4	5	6

G	H	I	J	K	L
7	8	9	10	11	12

M	N	O	P	Q	R
13	14	15	16	17	18

S	T	U	V	W	X
19	20	21	22	23	24

Y	Z
25	26

You be the scientist.

Alex's horse blows on a dandelion and makes a wish (to explore the savanna someday and meet a llama). Three months later, the horse sees new dandelions sprouting nearby. **WHAT HAPPENED?** Write your guess below.

DRAW A SEQUENCE of pictures in the boxes below showing what you think happened:

What are **SOME WAYS THAT SEEDS CAN TRAVEL** and make new plants? Circle the correct answer(s).

A. they float away on water

B. they blow away in the wind

C. animals carry them in their bodies or on their fur

D. all of the above

LABEL THE FOUR PARTS OF THIS PLANT:

ROOTS, LEAVES, FLOWER, STEM

CHARTING DATA

These mobs are right at the end of a very exciting race. **HOW LONG WILL IT TAKE FOR EACH MOB TO GET TO THE FINISH LINE?**

The **ENDERMAN** teleports in 1 second to the finish line of this race.

The **GHAST** takes 9 seconds longer than the Enderman.

The **SKELETON** gets to the finish line in 5 seconds.

RECORD EACH RACER'S TIME ON THE CHART.

ADD YOUR OWN NAME and (imaginary) time to the chart.

DRAW YOURSELF IN THE RACE according to the time you wrote in the chart.

Name	Time
Enderman	1 second
Ghast	
Skeleton	

Minecrafters know all about **BLOCKS.** They use different kinds of blocks to **BUILD FUN SHELTERS AND STRUCTURES,** and they break blocks to gather resources (like redstone!).

In Your Words

Why do you think Minecrafters build with blocks instead of triangular pyramids?

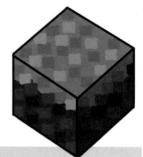

A Minecraft block is shaped like a cube. A **CUBE** is a **THREE-DIMENSIONAL SHAPE** with 6 sides (or faces). Find your way through the faces of the purpur block cube below.

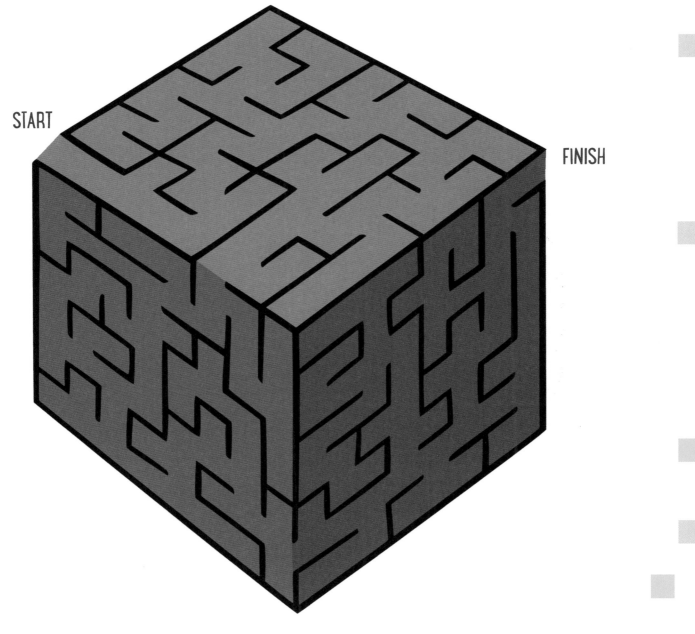

START

FINISH

You can see three faces (or sides) of this redstone ore block.
HOW MANY FACES ARE HIDDEN FROM VIEW?

ANSWER: _____

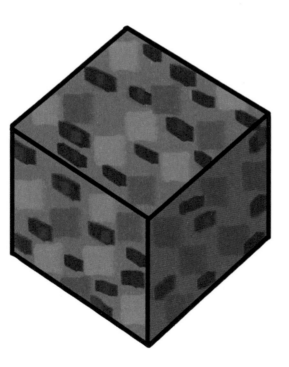

Look at the 2-dimensional shapes below.

WHICH ONE CAN BE CUT OUT AND FOLDED TO MAKE A CUBE?

If it helps, you can trace them onto white paper and try folding them yourself!

A.

B.

C.

I CAN'T DECIDE "WITHER" IT'S A, B, OR C. I FEEL LIKE SUCH A BLOCKHEAD!

THINK LIKE AN ENGINEER

DESIGN A PEN FOR A MINECRAFT COW. Include at least one machine in your pen. Use buttons, levers, redstone, pressure plates, stairs, or anything else that exists in the game.

SOME IDEAS FOR MACHINES:

1. A machine that allows the animal to feed itself when Alex is gone for a long time.

   OR

2. A machine that detects, or protects the animal, from approaching hostile mobs.

   OR

3. A machine that's all your idea!

MEASUREMENTS: COMPARING SIZES

Look at the hostile mobs below. Read the clues at right to **FIND OUT HOW TALL EACH MOB IS.** Write the measurements (to the closet half inch) on the lines. Check them with a ruler.

Mob	Height (in inches)
WITHER	
SPIDER	
ENDERMAN	
SKELETON	

Clues

1. One of the mobs is **TWICE AS TALL** as two of the mobs. Who is it?

2. Two of the mobs are **½ INCH TALL.** Who are they?

Super Brain Buster

3. IF THE MOBS CAME TO LIFE, and they all became twice as big, how big would the tallest mob (the 3-headed wither) be?

Look at Steve's garden. He is planting three crops on his farm: **BEETROOT, MELON,** and **WHEAT.**

Each row of his farm has a different pattern.

FIGURE OUT THE PATTERN OF THE CROPS BELOW.

Then draw what is missing in the blank space.

1.  _____

2. 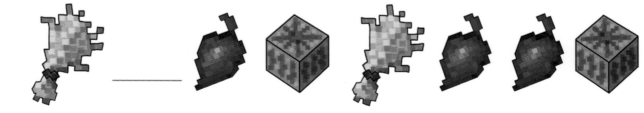 _____

3.  _____

MAKE A HYPOTHESIS

Steve planted this flower, **BUT IT'S STARTING TO WILT.**

What do you already know about plants and how they grow?
WRITE 3 THINGS YOU KNOW BELOW:

1.

2.

3.

SC**I**ENCE TALK

A **HYPOTHESIS** is a guess that you make using what you already know.

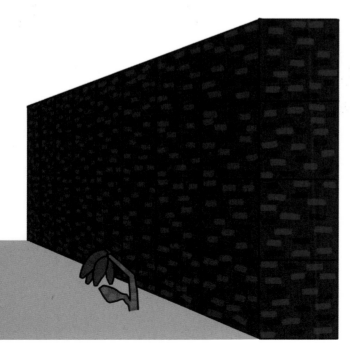

Make a hypothesis.
WHY IS THE FLOWER DYING?

WHAT CAN STEVE DO TO HELP THE FLOWER GROW?

SOFTWARE ENGINEERS WRITE CODE that tells the computer what to do when you type in a command.

COMMANDS like the ones in the chart to the right make something cool happen for Minecrafters like you.

Which of the commands listed on the next page would you type if you were battling the Ender dragon and didn't have the right weapon to defeat it?

WRITE IT HERE EXACTLY AS IT APPEARS ON THE CHART.

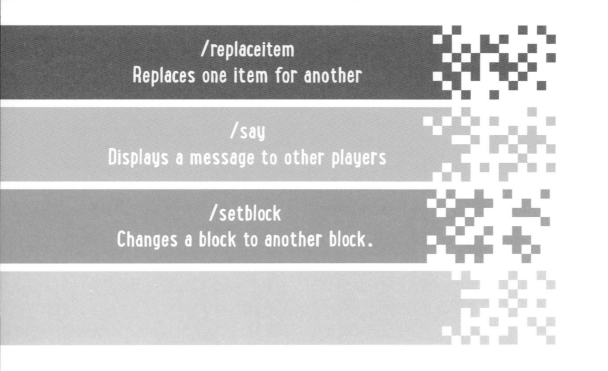

/replaceitem
Replaces one item for another

/say
Displays a message to other players

/setblock
Changes a block to another block.

PRETEND THAT YOU ARE A SOFTWARE ENGINEER and you want to create a new command for players to use in Minecraft.

WHAT COMMAND WOULD YOU CREATE? Write it on the chart in the light blue space.

WHY DID YOU CHOOSE THIS COMMAND?

FLOWER SCIENCE

When a bee drinks nectar from a flower, pollen can stick to its furry legs. When the bee visits another flower of the same kind, it carries the pollen with it. This act of **cross pollination** is one way that baby flowers, or seedlings, get made.

Bees + Pollen = Baby flowers!

Without bees, there would be fewer flowers in the world.

Only one of these bees drank from two flowers of the same kind. **FIND THE BEE THAT IS A CROSS POLLINATOR** by tracing each bee's path from beginning to end. The bee whose path crosses two similar flowers is the cross pollinator!

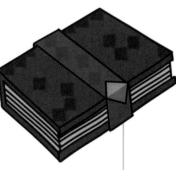

WORD UP

POLLEN: a powdery substance that a flower makes. Flowers make pollen so they can reproduce (make new flowers).

When pollen travels from one flower to another, it's called **CROSS POLLINATION.**

WATER CURRENTS AND TRANSPORTATION

For centuries, people have used **RIVERS** and **CURRENTS** to transport building materials and other useful resources.

ALEX WANTS TO USE THE RIVER to transport her valuable resources. She has a boat, but no oars. She'll have to go with the flow and let the **WATER CURRENT** carry her down this river so she can stash her **VALUABLE DIAMOND ARMOR** safely in a chest.

HELP ALEX FOLLOW THE WATER CURRENT TO TRANSPORT HER ARMOR SAFELY TO THE CHEST.

START

PHYSICAL PROPERTIES: MAKING OBSERVATIONS

Pretend you are a **MINECRAFTING SCIENTIST** observing items in the game and recording information about each item.

FILL IN THE OBSERVATION CHART BELOW:

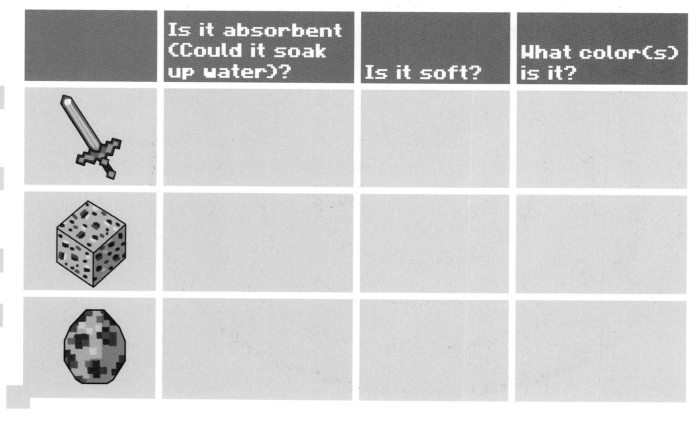

	Is it absorbent (Could it soak up water)?	Is it soft?	What color(s) is it?

NUMBER THE MATERIALS BELOW IN ORDER FROM SOFTEST (1) TO HARDEST (3).

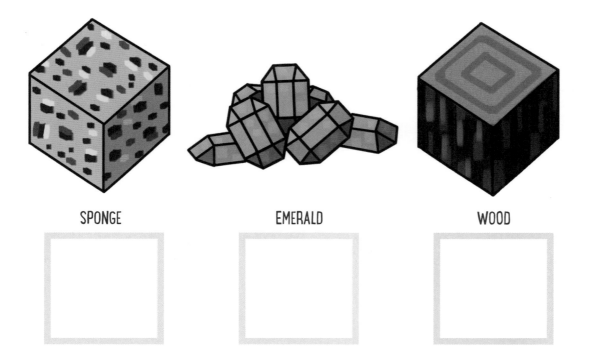

SPONGE

EMERALD

WOOD

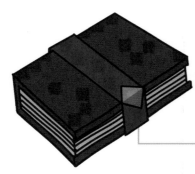

WORD UP

OBSERVATION: something you notice when you examine or test an object

PHYSICAL PROPERTIES

Look around the room and **IDENTIFY THREE DIFFERENT ITEMS.** Add their names to the numbered spaces on the chart below.

Now think of a **CHARACTERISTIC** to observe. Write a describing word (like **SQUISHY, SMALL, SHARP, OR FURRY**) in the second column on the top of the chart and answer *yes* or *no* for each item.

A **CHARACTERISTIC** is something that describes an item and makes it different from other items.

Item Name	Characteristic: Is this item _____?
1.	
2.	
3.	

FRACTIONS AND MORE

Look at the items you gathered in your **INVENTORY!**
Use your **MATH SKILLS** to answer the questions.

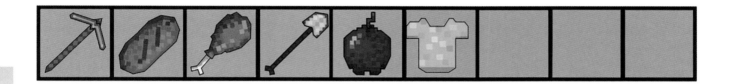

1. How many items do you have in total?

2. How many of those items can you eat?

3. What fraction shows how many of your
total items you can eat.

a) ⁴⁄₆   b) ³⁄₆   c) ³⁄₇

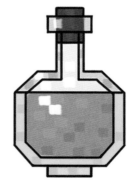

4. Put a star above the one item in your inventory that you can wear.

5. Draw 3 new kinds of food to fill your inventory bar.

6. After lots of mining, your tools broke! Cross out all of the tools in your inventory bar.

7. How many items do you have in your inventory now?

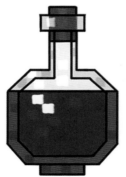 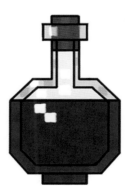

ALGEBRA: SOLVING FOR X IN MINECRAFTING

Algebra is all about **SOLVING A MYSTERY.** What mystery number is missing from the equation below?

WRITE IT ON THE LINE.

$$\underline{\hspace{2cm}} + 1 = 4$$

MINECRAFTERS USE FORMULAS to craft items in the game. For example, they need to know the ingredients and the formula for making milk if they want to reverse the effect of a bad potion.

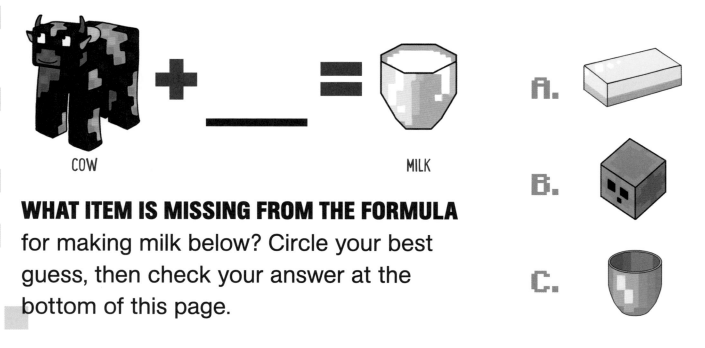

COW   MILK

A.

B.

C.

WHAT ITEM IS MISSING FROM THE FORMULA for making milk below? Circle your best guess, then check your answer at the bottom of this page.

Here is a formula for **CRAFTING POTION OF WATER BREATHING** in Minecraft.

AWKWARD POTION   PUFFERFISH   POTION OF WATER BREATHING

Potion Formula Challenge

Use the formula for potion of Water Breathing above to solve these algebraic formulas. **DRAW OR WRITE IN WHAT IS MISSING.**

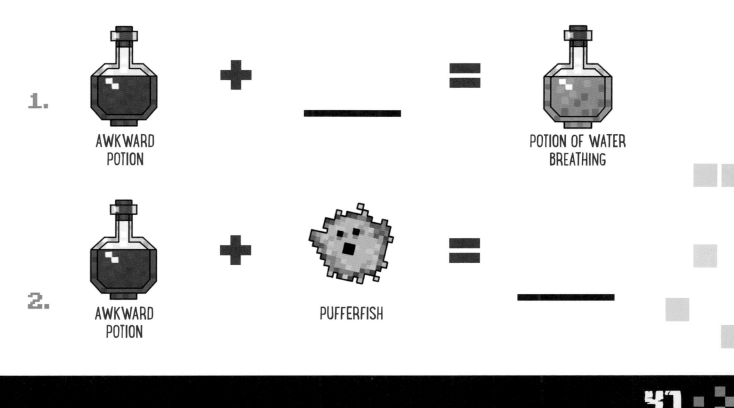

1. AWKWARD POTION + _____ = POTION OF WATER BREATHING

2. AWKWARD POTION + PUFFERFISH = _____

OBSERVING AND USING YOUR ENVIRONMENT

There are lots of different **BIOMES** to explore in Minecraft. Each one has its own landforms, features, and water formations.

Look at the two different biomes pictured here. Write what you **OBSERVE** and **HYPOTHESIZE** about each biome.

Cold Taiga Biome

One thing I notice about this biome is

It would be a good place to

Swampland

One thing I notice about this biome is

It would be a good place to

MY WORLD

DRAW YOURSELF in the biome of your choice and **DESCRIBE TWO ACTIVITIES** you would like to do in that environment.

ACTIVITIES I WOULD LIKE TO DO HERE:

1.

2.

3.

MAP MAKING

Steve is exploring the Taiga M biome and it's **CRAWLING WITH CREEPERS.** He needs a map to help him get resources and hide from the creepers.

Use the space below to **DRAW A MAP FOR STEVE.**

- ◆ Draw 6 triangles on this map on the far right to show mountains.

- ◆ Draw a column of trees down the center of the map. They can look like lowercase "t"s.

- ◆ Draw a big lake to the left of the trees.

- ◆ Draw 10 rectangles all around the map to reveal the location of the creepers. (These can be placed anywhere!)

BINARY CODE

Computers think and respond to binary code. Binary code is a **NUMERIC SYSTEM MADE UP OF ONLY TWO NUMBERS, 0 AND 1,** but those two numbers can communicate a lot more information than you think!

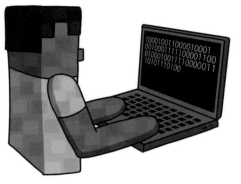

You can think of binary code this way:

0 MEANS OFF.

1 MEANS ON.

Look at these torches. We can use binary code to represent a lit torch and an unlit torch (or stick).

Use 0 to represent an unlit torch. Use 1 for a lit torch.

WRITE THE CORRECT NUMBER NEXT TO EACH ITEM BELOW.

THIS SWITCH can activate a creeper trap and squish a creeper. When the switch is in the up position, the trap is off.

If the switch points down, the trap is on, and creepers better watch out!

LOOK AT THE SERIES OF SWITCHES BELOW and write the number 0 on the line if the switch is up (off) and 1 on the line if the switch is down (on).

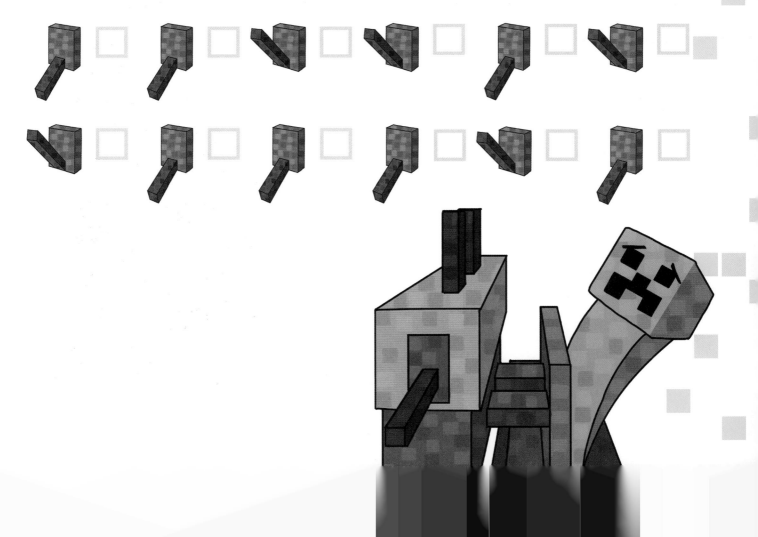

WRITE YOUR BIRTHDAY IN BINARY CODE!

Use the chart on the next page to write your birthday in computer language.

WRITE YOUR BIRTHDAY THE REGULAR WAY HERE.

_ _ / _ _ / _ _

Now look at the chart on the next page and **WRITE YOUR BIRTHDAY IN BINARY CODE!**

ARE YOU OLDER OR YOUNGER THAN STEVE?

Steve's birthday is **5/17/09.**

He would write his birthday in binary code like this:

101100011001

number	binary code	number	binary code
0	0	16	10000
1	01	17	10001
2	10	18	10010
3	11	19	10011
4	100	20	10100
5	101	21	10101
6	110	22	10110
7	111	23	10111
8	1000	24	11000
9	1001	25	11001
10	1010	26	11010
11	1011	27	11011
12	1100	28	11100
13	1101	29	11101
14	1110	30	11110
15	1111	31	11111

MATTER IS ANYTHING THAT TAKES UP SPACE AND HAS MASS. The cereal you ate this morning is matter; the bowl it was served in is matter; and the milk you poured on top is matter!

All matter can be described as a **SOLID, LIQUID,** or **GAS.** Those are the three states of matter.

GET THIS!

MATTER CAN CHANGE FROM ONE STATE TO ANOTHER! Liquid can freeze and turn to a solid. A liquid can also evaporate and turn to gas. Gases can condense and turn to liquid (think of a heavy cloud turning to rain!).

LOOK AT THE MINECRAFTING PICTURES BELOW.

Each one shows matter.

 CIRCLE all of the liquids.

✱ **STAR** the solids.

✔ Make a **CHECKMARK** next to any gases.

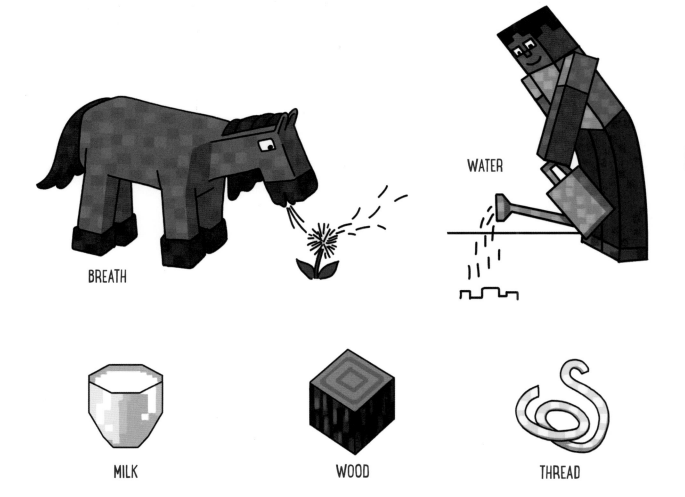

BREATH

WATER

MILK

WOOD

THREAD

LOOK AROUND YOU. What do you see? What is invisible, but you know it's there? Try to fill the chart below with real-life examples of each kind of matter.

Liquid	Solid	Gas

NOT SURE WHAT KIND OF MATTER IT IS? USE THESE CLUES.

LIQUID: Takes the shape of its container.

SOLID: Keeps its shape the same no matter the container.

GAS: Often invisible. Can float or move around.

Add a Resource

Choose a real-life solid, liquid, or gas to add to your inventory in Minecraft. How could it help you build or survive?

MY IDEA:

HOW IT'S USEFUL:

NOT ALL GASES ARE INVISIBLE.
Chlorine gas is yellowy green and iodine gas is dark purple!

CALCULATING AN ESCAPE

ALEX AND HER FRIENDS NEED TO CROSS THIS RED-HOT LAVA PIT to escape a group of attacking zombies. An obsidian boat is the only thing that can help them get safely to the other side.

Each boat holds 2 creatures.

HOW MANY BOATS DOES ALEX NEED TO CRAFT to save herself and all of her friends?

DRAW THE BOATS THEY'LL NEED HERE.

Magma and lava both describe hot, liquid rock. Below the Earth's surface, we call this molten rock **MAGMA**. When it rises above the surface, to where we can see it, it's called **LAVA**.

AND SURVIVAL

THE ARCTIC TUNDRA IS COLD. One animal that lives there is the polar bear.

1. Circle another animal that lives in the artic.

2. Why is it good to have white fur if you live in the arctic?

LANDFORMS AND EROSION

The wind is very strong in the arctic tundra. If it blows on this mountain for years and years, the strong wind will start to **WEATHER** (wear away) and **ERODE** (carry away pieces of) the mountain. Trees, bushes, plants, or tall grass can protect the mountain from this kind of erosion.

DRAW A WALL OF GRASS, PLANTS, AND/OR TREES to help keep the wind from eroding this mountain below.

DID YOU KNOW?

WIND and **WATER** can change the shape of land over time. Flowing water can carve a deep valley between mountains. Wind can make mountains smaller and make the land flatter.

Deductive Reasoning

Engineering and Design
Answer: C

Code Cracker: Enchanted Chest
SIGNS AND LADDERS

Plant Science
The seeds on the flower were carried away in the air and landed where they started to grow new flowers.

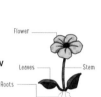

Answer: D

Math Fun Run: Charting Data
Enderman: 1 second, Ghast: 10 seconds, Skeleton: 5 seconds

Block Party
Answers may vary, but cubes are easier to stack and make buildings that are pretty secure, even when they're tall!

New Dimensions in Geometry
Three faces are hidden from view.

Answer: A

Measurement: Comparing Sizes
Wither: 1 ½ inches
Spider and Enderman: ½ inches
Skeleton: 1 inch

Clues
1. Skeleton
2. Spider and Enderman
3. 3 inches

Math Patterns
1. melon
2. wheat
3. beetroot

Science: Make a Hypothesis
Answers may vary, but plants need sun, water, air (carbon dioxide) and nutrients from the soil to grow.

Computer Commands
/replaceitem

Flower Science
Bee C is the cross-pollinator.

Water Currents and Transportation

Physical Properties: Making Observations

	Is it absorbent (Could it soak up water)?	Is it soft?	What color(s) is it?
(sword)	No	No	Blue
(sponge)	Yes	Yes	Yellow
(egg)	No	No	Pink

1, 3, 2

Fractions and More
1. 6
2. 3
3. b
4.
5) Answers may vary.
6.
7. 7

Algebra: Solving for X in Minecrafting
1. X = pufferfish
2. X= potion of Water Breathing

Observing and Using Your Environment
Answers may vary.

Map Making
(Answers may vary.)

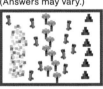

Binary Code

0   1

1.   110010
2.   011101

States of Matter

Calculating an Escape
3 boats

Animals and Survival
1. (sheep)

2. It's good to have white fur so you can stay warm, blend into the snow, and hide from predators.